WRITE THE STORY THAT COULD MAKE YOU RICH:

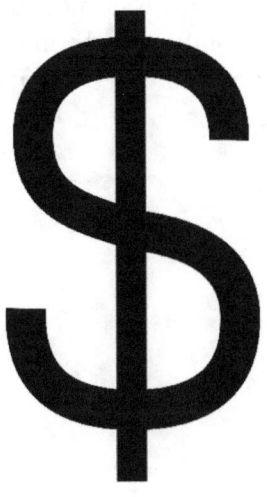

THE FORMULA USED TO WRITE THE TOP-GROSSING FILMS AND BOOKS

PAUL LARKIN

TABLE of CONTENTS

Introduction

FINDING and SUMMARISING the FIVE TOP-GROSSING FILMS and BOOKS
Chapter 1: Which are the five top-grossing films and books of all time?
Chapter 2: A quick summary of the five top-grossing films and books.

DISCOVER COMMON ELEMENTS in the FIVE TOP-GROSSING FILMS and BOOKS
Chapter 3: What do all the top-grossing films and books have in common?

WHAT is the FORMULA for a QUICK, BASIC STORY?
Chapter 4: A possible formula that will get you started.

JUST DO IT – CREATE a VERY QUICK and BASIC STORY
Chapter 5: Create a quick, basic story – where do you get ideas?
Chapter 6: Some examples of quick, basic stories.

CREATE a BEGINNING
Chapter 7: Now that you've finished – let's begin.

YOU'VE GOT the BASICS – NOW ELABORATE:
CHARACTERS, MOTIVES + GOALS + ACTIONS
Chapter 8: Characters: Bad and Good.
Chapter 9: Characters: Are you Air, Fire, Water, or Earth?

Chapter 10: Characters: Horoscope.
Chapter 11: Motivation: Goals and Action.
Chapter 12: Motivation: The Seven Deadly Sins.
Chapter 13: Motivation: The Five Needs.

WHY YOUR AUDIENCE JUST HAS to PAY ATTENTION
Chapter 14: What has death got to do with storytelling?
Chapter 15: Other ways to get the attention of your audience.
Chapter 16: A quick tour of the brain, and why your audience will pay attention.

CONCLUSION
Chapter 17: The end … not really: every story needs something extra.

References

INTRODUCTION

WHY I WROTE THIS BOOK

My strongest skills are in public speaking and presenting. The presentation gurus are constantly emphasising the use of stories when addressing an audience. While I knew some entertaining stories, I never knew why they captivated my audience.

And so started my quest. I wanted to know why certain stories fascinated people. I wanted to know the combination of elements that would enchant my audience so that I, too, could hypnotise my listeners with a spellbinding story.

At first I read everything and anything that mentioned creating a great story. Some authors stressed knowing the characters. Others spoke of plot structure and organising events. The setting was important for some books, while the use of descriptive words was advocated by other writers.

With all this knowledge you'd think I'd be brilliant, and my stories would be published in every popular magazine. This was not the case. Instead, I got more and more depressed. I felt totally incompetent. One author told me to do this and another suggested I do that. Every book about writing seemed to know what was vital to a good story. At one point I was so totally confused that I almost gave up my dream. My dream was to know the elements of a great story so that I could create stories that would cast a spell on my audience. It wasn't happening.

One day the idea hit me. It seemed so obvious. It was just one sentence, but it started me on this journey. The idea that had this power was this: analyse the stories in the five top-grossing books and films and just list what happened in them. In theory this should discover the elements of a great story, a story that was so good that people would pay money to see or read it.

And that is how this book came about. Join me as I journey through this analysis and see if you agree with the findings.

WHY YOU SHOULD READ THIS BOOK

You too may have read many books on how to write a dynamic story. Like me, you were left with a feeling of, 'Where should I start?' One author promotes this strategy, another tells us to get into the habit of doing that, while some authors regurgitate what other authors advised. We follow them blindly, thinking they are the experts. But we produce nothing ourselves. The people getting richer are the authors of the books on how to write, while we get poorer and poorer and produce nothing.

If this sounds like you, then this is the book that should get your creative juices flowing and may help you to produce a story that could make you rich.

In this book there is no 'do this' or 'do that'. There is none of the supercilious advice telling you the way a story should be written. The analysis you will meet is based on facts. It is an examination of the five top-grossing films and books of all time. These lucky writers discovered and used a formula that captivated the attention of millions of human beings. These authors/writers knew a secret. They knew and used a formula. A formula that resonates in all successful stories.

The analysis and findings in the pages you will now read could help give you the confidence to write the masterpiece that you are capable of. It may help you write the story that could make you rich.

FINDING and SUMMARISING the five top-grossing films and books

CHAPTER 1

Which are the five top-grossing films and books of all time?

If we are to know the elements of a top-grossing story it is appropriate that we should first discover which stories are global phenomena. The top-grossing films and books of all time are stories that millions of people have paid money to see or read. These stories were not free. People had to go to a cinema or a bookstore or fill in a form online to access them. They had to do something before anything happened, and it involved their money. If we analyse these stories we might find a formula which produces stories that the world wants to experience.

In this chapter you will discover which films and books form the list of the five top-grossing films and books.

FILMS

If you type 'The five top-grossing films worldwide' into Google the results will always include a combination of:

Avatar
Titanic
Star Wars: The Force Awakens
Jurassic Park
The Avengers Assemble

BOOKS

If you type 'The five top-grossing fiction books worldwide' into Google the results will always include a combination of:

The Lord of the Rings
The Hobbit
The Little Prince
Harry Potter and the Philosopher's Stone
And Then There Were None

Why use the top-grossing films and books in the quest to find the magic formula? Because people have paid money to see or read these works. People feel that these masterpieces are so good that they were willing to pay to experience them. They did not just download a freebie. They used the money they earned to pay for the film or the book. They were serious about viewing the product.

CHAPTER 2
A quick summary of the five top-grossing films and books

In this chapter we will look at a synopsis of each film and book.

FILMS

Avatar
A mining company wants to drive off the native Na'vi tribe in order to mine the precious material scattered throughout its territory. The colonel plans his extermination tactics, and this forces Jake to take a stand. Jake fights back in an epic battle for the fate of Pandora, in which many are killed.

Titanic
American Jack Dawson spots the society girl Rose DeWitt Bukater. Rose is accompanied by her rich, snobbish fiancé, Caledon Hockley. They are on their way to America to get married. Rose feels helplessly trapped by her situation. When Rose attempts suicide, by jumping off the stern, Jack pulls her back and a bond is forged between them. Caledon Hockley uses desperate measures to keep them apart. But that strategy fails when the *Titanic* collides with an iceberg. Jack dies and Rose survives.

Star Wars: The Force Awakens
The First Order attempts to rule the galaxy by killing any opposition. A desperate group of heroes tries to stop them, along with the help of the Resistance. After many explosions and deaths Rey and her companions defeat the First Order.

Jurassic Park

On a remote island a wealthy entrepreneur secretly creates a theme park featuring living dinosaurs created from prehistoric DNA. However, the park's security system breaks down and the prehistoric creatures break out and start eating the humans. The invited guests fight for survival.

The Avengers Assemble

When global security is threatened by the evil Loki and his followers Nick Fury and his team need all their powers to save the world from disaster and death.

BOOKS

In this section we will look at a synopsis of each book.

The Lord of the Rings

A young hobbit named Frodo is chosen to destroy the One Ring. This was created by the dark lord, Sauron, who threatens to kill all opposition. Frodo is assigned warriors including Gandalf, Aragorn, and Boromir. It will not be an easy journey for the Fellowship of the Ring, whose members are on the ultimate quest to rid Middle-Earth of all evil.

The Hobbit

A reluctant hobbit sets out to the Lonely Mountain with a group of dwarves to reclaim their mountain home – and the gold within it – from the dragon Smaug. Smaug is determined to defend his possession, and will kill all intruders.

The Little Prince

A pilot crashes in the barren Sahara Desert. He is close to death. A prince suddenly appears from the planet Asteroid B-

612. In the days that follow the pilot learns of the small boy's history and his planet-hopping journeys, in which he met a king, a businessman, a historian, and a general. It isn't until the Little Prince comes to Earth that he learns the secrets of the importance of life from a fox, a snake, and the pilot.

Harry Potter and the Philosopher's Stone
Voldemort killed Harry's parents. Harry goes to a school for wizards. He and his companions soon learn that something very valuable is hidden somewhere inside the school. Voldemort is very anxious to lay his hands on it. He tries to kill Harry, but Harry survives.

And Then There Were None
Ten people are invited to a hotel, only to find that an unseen person is killing them one by one. Who is the killer?

In the following chapters you will use these films and books in your quest to find the formula that makes a top-grossing story.

DISCOVERING
COMMON ELEMENTS
in the five top-grossing films and books

CHAPTER 3

What do all the top-grossing films and books have in common?

You have looked at the five top-grossing films and books. Can you now draw any conclusions about what you should include in your blockbuster story?

DEATH

The first thing that struck me about the films was that all of them involved death.

In *Avatar* it was the death of Jake and lots of Na'vis and lots of troopers. In *Titanic* poor Jack and hundreds of passengers died. *Star Wars: The Force Awakens* depicted many battles and killings. *Jurassic World* had dinosaurs eating humans. And *The Avengers Assemble* saw evil beings killing humans by the dozen.

The common factor in all the books is death. *The Lord of the Rings* has many battles and death scenes. *The Hobbit* sees Bilbo facing frequent encounters with death. *The Little Prince* has a pilot who may die as he crashes in the desert. *Harry Potter and the Philosopher's Stone* starts with the announcement of the death of Harry's parents and continues with the threats of death by trolls and the three dogs. *And Then There Were None* has a series of chapters devoted to death.

It would seem that if you want to write a top-grossing story you should include death.

EVIL

In all the top-grossing films and books evil initiates the action. *Avatar* starts with the corporation organising the obliteration of the Na'vis in order to mine the precious material. *Titanic* has the wicked fiancé humiliating poor Rose, so that she is determined to commit suicide. *Star Wars: The Force Awakens* begins with the First Order destroying everyone who opposes its objective. *Jurassic World* has the dinosaurs killing the humans. *The Avengers Assemble* tells how Loki uses his powers to obtain the elixir of life and destroys anything that opposes him. *The Lord of the Rings* is based on the fact that the rings were made by the evil Smaug, along with his intention to control the universe through violence and murder. *The Hobbit* has the mighty dragon taking over the home of the hobbits and being prepared to kill any opposition. *The Little Prince* starts with the plane crashing and the pilot almost dying. *Harry Potter and the Philosopher's Stone* is prefaced by the murder of his parents by the evil Voldemort and then his frequent skirmishes with the children. *And Then There Were None* is a smorgasbord of murders initiated by an evil one.

If you want to write a top-grossing story it appears that you should begin with an evil character doing something evil.

FANTASY

Four out of the five top-grossing films have places, people, costumes, objects … anything and everything … that is totally imaginary. *Avatar* has huge aliens in a land of strange plants. *Star Wars: The Force Awakens* introduces us to a weird collection of interplanetary beings. *Jurassic World* shows dinosaurs as present-day creatures. *The Avengers Assemble* is a mixture of legends and humans who have supernatural powers.

The top-grossing books tell the same tale about fantasy. Four out of five of these stories have totally imaginary elements. *The Lord of the Rings* is set in a past time in an imaginary location, and shows us supernatural powers. *The Hobbit* shows characters and beings that do not exist in our world. *The Little Prince* is totally out of this world, as we visit the prince's universe. *Harry Potter and the Philosopher's Stone* has broomsticks and spells, strange creatures, and the supernatural.

To earn the top financial rewards for your story it would seem that you should include lots of fantasy.

REALITY

As regards films the odd one out is *Titanic*. This contains real people, believable circumstances, and everyday objects. So, if reality is your thing, you can definitely write stories that will make you rich.

Now let us look at the odd one out concerning books. *And Then There Were None* is the only top-grossing book that has no strange creatures or alien planets. All the characters are human, and the setting is on Planet Earth … on an island … in a house. No CGI was used in the writing of this book.

To earn the top financial rewards for your story it would seem this formula of reality can produce a top-grossing book or film and made you very rich.

CHARACTERS

In all the films and books the main characters always have human characteristics. To be more specific, these characters always have the variety of characteristics that depict the character as a human being. I'm thinking of *The Little Prince* with his curiosity. The characters of *The Avengers Assemble* may have special powers, but they also have those qualities of care that are common to humans. *Titanic* shows a man in love with a woman. *Avatar* may have converted a human being into a strange alien, but the emotions are still those of a human falling in love with a mate and then wanting to protect his tribe (the reciprocating emotions of the alien being are surprisingly human). *The Lord of the Rings*, *The Hobbit*, and all the other top-grossing films and books have characters who have all the emotions of human beings.

Surprisingly, the evil characters in the top-grossing films and books have the same characteristics as human beings but the characters come in different shapes and sizes. The films *Avatar*, *Star Wars: The Force Awakens*, *The Avengers Assemble*, and *Titanic* have an evil character who wants to be all-powerful. In *Avatar* it is a human being, but it is a spirit being in both *Star Wars: The Force Awakens* and *The Avengers Assemble*. Even *Jurassic World* suggests that the evil animals want to conquer the humans and rule the island. It is a similar finding in books. The evil character may not be human, but it does have human emotions and human motivation.

It would seem that to write a top-grossing film or book you should include main characters who have human qualities.

GOALS

In all top-grossing films and books the BAD has one goal, and is continually striving for the attainment of that one goal. The GOOD has many goals. The goal is the 'what' of the story. It answers the question, 'What does the BAD want?' and the question 'What does the GOOD want?'

There is more about goals in the chapter on motivation (Chapter 11: Motivation: Goals and Action). It is sufficient to say at this point that your story must have an evil character who wants something – usually to harm the good character.

MOTIVATION

In all the top-grossing films and books the main characters are motivated to achieve their goals. For the BAD and the GOOD it is their life-or-death determination to succeed that makes these stories so compelling. The motivation answers the question 'why?' 'Why does the BAD want this?' 'Why does the GOOD want this?' There is more about motivation in a later chapter.

While you are generating ideas for your story just guess a possible motive for the evil character as it tries to harm the good character.

ACTION

Each story is littered with episodes that demonstrate BAD's action as it moves towards its one specific goal. The actions are the 'how?' of the story. Meanwhile, GOOD has many mini goals and survives each – despite opposition from many mini BADs.

There is more about survival in the chapter on death (Chapter 14: What has death got to do with storytelling?). It is sufficient to say at this point that your story must have an evil character who has one goal, and all the character's actions are focused on achieving that one goal. The good character opposes the evil character in some scenes. However, in others the good character has other goals and other motivations.

ENDINGS: HAPPY

In three out of the five top-grossing films the ending is happy. Good defeats evil. *Star Wars: The Force Awakens* sees the Resistance defeating the First Order. *Jurassic World* ends with the humans dominating the animals. *The Avengers Assemble* shows our characters subduing Loki and saving the world.

Four out of the top-grossing books end on a happy note. The *Lord of the Rings* has Frodo involved in destroying the ring. *The Hobbit* ends with a successful event as the dwarves reclaim their homeland. *The Little Prince* concludes with the prince knowing what friendship is. *Harry Potter and the Philosopher's Stone* shows Harry frustrating the evil Voldemort's intentions.

ENDINGS: SAD

Two of the five top-grossing films have a sad ending. *Avatar* shows us Jake dying as he unites with the Sacred Tree. *Titanic* sees a relationship ending as Jack drowns and Rose is left alone. If you like sad endings you can still write stories that will make you rich.

Only one book has a sad ending. *And Then There Were None* has numerous murders, and even the murderer dies. The guests themselves never discovered who the murderer was. Here there is proof that you can indeed write a top-grossing story with a sad ending.

CONCLUSION: All top-grossing films and books contain these elements:

- Death
- Evil initiates the action
- Fantasy (four out of five)
- Characters have the qualities of human beings
- Evil has one goal, one motivation, and evil actions
- GOOD is involved in many mini episodes that may or may not relate to the ultimate goal
- Each GOOD mini episode has its own goal, motivation, and actions
- The ending can either be happy (GOOD wins) or sad (BAD wins).

What seems to be the FORMULA for a quick, basic story?

CHAPTER 4
A possible formula that will get you started

If we take the bare bones of the story in each film there seems to be a common pattern.

- The evil character (BAD) does (action) something (goal) to harm the good character (GOOD).
- Deep down, there is a reason (motivation) why BAD does this.
- The good character (GOOD) reacts and wants to defeat BAD.
- GOOD is involved in many mini episodes that may or may not relate to the ultimate goal.
- Each GOOD mini episode has its own goal, motivation, and actions.
- GOOD finally wins (GOOD can lose).

FILMS

Star Wars: The Force Awakens
The First Order attempts to rule the galaxy and only a ragtag group of heroes can stop them, along with the help of the Resistance.

BAD does something evil = the First Order has renewed its attacks on the Resistance.

BAD's reason (motivation) = to rule the universe.

GOOD reacts (Examples plus more examples not related to the ultimate aim)

- Rey (a scavenger), Finn and BB-8 (a robot) escape a First Order raid in an old spaceship belonging to Hans Solo.
- Rey impresses Hans with her engineering knowledge.
- Rey goes with them to a cantina (run by Maz Kanata) where they find Skywalker's lightsabre and then escape another First Order attack.
- Rey is captured by the First Order.
- Rey is rescued by Finn and Hans Solo.

GOOD perseveres and wins =
Rey and the Resistance destroy the First Order's base

Avatar
A greedy corporate figurehead intends to exterminate the natives (the Na'vi) in order to mine for the precious material scattered throughout their rich woodland. The restless colonel moves forward with his ruthless extermination tactics, forcing Jake to take a stand – and fight back in an epic battle for the fate of Pandora.

BAD does something evil = the colonel wants to exterminate the natives.

BAD's reason (motivation) = to obtain the highly prized material.

GOOD reacts (Examples plus more examples not related to the ultimate aim)
- Jake is to persuade the Na'vi to move to another area.
- Jake is seen in sequences where he learns to be a Na'vi.
- Jake falls in love with Neytiri and they marry.

- Jake fights the colonel when he attacks but has to retreat.
- Jake gathers the other Na'vi tribes to resist the colonel.

GOOD perseveres and wins =
Jake and the Na'vi overthrow the colonel.

Jurassic World
On a remote island a wealthy entrepreneur secretly creates a theme park featuring living dinosaurs drawn from prehistoric DNA. However, the park's security system breaks down and the prehistoric creatures break out. The invited guests fight for survival.

BAD does something evil = *Indominus rex* dinosaur hunts humans

BAD's reason (motivation) = to return to their natural habitat

GOOD reacts (Examples plus more examples not related to the ultimate aim)
- Owen trains velociraptors and rescues helper.
- Owen detects *Indominus* is still in the pen and then escapes from it.
- Owen flirts with Claire.
- Owen rescues boys after the pod episode.
- Owen, Claire, and boys are chased by *Indominus*.

GOOD perseveres and wins =
Owen gets other velociraptors to turn on *Indominus* and kill it.

The Avengers Assemble
When global security is threatened by Loki and his followers Nick Fury and his team need all their powers to save the world from disaster.

BAD does something evil = Loki captures an extraterrestrial energy source.

BAD's reason (motivation) = to subjugate Earth.

GOOD reacts (Examples plus more examples not related to the ultimate aim)
- Nick Fury gathers a team of superheroes.
- Nick captures Loki but Loki escapes.
- Nick saves Manhattan from bomb.

GOOD perseveres and wins =
Nick and the Avengers destroy Loki and his army.

BOOKS

If we take the bare bones of the story in each book there seems to be a common pattern.

- The evil character (BAD) does (action) something (goal) to harm the good character (GOOD).
- Deep down, there is a reason (motivation) why BAD does this.
- The good character (GOOD) reacts and wants to defeat BAD.
- GOOD is involved in many mini episodes that may or may not relate to the ultimate goal.

- Each GOOD mini episode has its own goal, motivation, and actions.
- GOOD finally wins (GOOD can lose).

Harry Potter and the Philosopher's Stone
Voldemort killed Harry's parents. Harry and companions soon learn that something very valuable is hidden somewhere inside the school. Voldemort is very anxious to lay his hands on it. He tries to kill Harry but Harry survives.

BAD does something evil = Voldemort kills Mr and Mrs Potter and tries to kill Harry.

BAD's reason (motivation) = wants the Philosopher's Stone so he can rule the universe.

GOOD reacts (Examples plus more examples not related to the ultimate aim)
- Harry almost killed during the Quidditch match but escapes spell.
- Harry tries to find out who has been killing unicorns and is attacked by a hooded man.
- Harry is attacked by Quirrell but survives.

GOOD perseveres and wins =
Harry prevents Voldemort from getting the Philosopher's Stone.

And Then There Were None
Ten people are invited to a hotel, only to find that an unseen person is killing them one by one. Who is the killer? They discover the killer.

BAD does something evil = a murderer wants to kill eight selected people.

BAD's reason (motivation) = to punish the guilty.

GOOD reacts (Examples plus more examples not related to the ultimate aim)
- Guests search the island for the murderer but find no one.
- Guests lock their doors at night but killer still commits murder.
- Guests lock away all murder weapons but murders continue.
- One guest goes missing but a search reveals nothing.
- All guests murdered but the killer is not found.

GOOD perseveres and wins =
A twist to the usual trend. The GOOD – in this case – is a person who wants justice. The BAD were the guests, who deserved death in the GOOD's eyes. The GOOD achieved his objective.

LET'S DO IT -
a very quick and basic story
plus
some examples

CHAPTER 5
Create a quick, basic story – where do you get ideas?

In this chapter you will learn how to quickly create a basic story that resembles a top-grossing film or book story.

You are now aware that a top-grossing story has the following elements:

- The evil character (BAD) does (action) something (goal) to harm the good character (GOOD).
- Deep down, there is a reason (motivation) why BAD does this.
- The good character (GOOD) reacts and wants to defeat BAD.
- GOOD is involved in many mini episodes that may or may not relate to the ultimate goal.
- Each GOOD mini episode has its own goal, motivation, and actions.
- GOOD finally wins.

At this point all we are concerned with is a situation that will produce an action from the BAD and reaction from the GOOD. You are now looking for ideas that suggest what BAD wants.

(We will deliberately leave the introduction until we have created this story. Only when we know the actions, the reactions, and the finale will we be able to create a suitable introduction.)

You will see in another chapter that BAD can be a person, a thing, nature, or an animal.

GOOD can also be a person, a thing, nature, or an animal.

Remember also that BAD will initiate the action. This is the only concern you should have for now. Choose BAD, then start.

You are looking for a situation which you can develop into examples of BAD acting and GOOD getting in the way.

So where do you find these examples?

The Tabloid Press

For me the tabloid press is a brilliant source of GOOD and BAD. I look for those little snippets which lead me to think that the journalist is making up the report. They are so unbelievable. I saw one article:

A father used to get drunk then disappear for weeks on end. On one occasion he was gone for five weeks. Meanwhile, his children sold the house, bought cars, and booked holidays.
(My fertile little mind went into overdrive.) The father returned. The children tried various ways to get rid of him. The son tried to kill him but failed. The son was sentenced to prison. The father moved into the son's house.

Seriously, you wouldn't believe it. But the tabloids give us some fabulous ideas for the BAD formula:
- The evil character (BAD) does (action) something (goal) to harm the good character (GOOD).
- Deep down, there is a reason (motivation) why BAD does this.
- The good character (GOOD) reacts and wants to defeat BAD.

- GOOD is involved in many mini episodes that may or may not relate to the ultimate goal.
- Each GOOD mini episode has its own goal, motivation, and actions.
- GOOD finally wins.

I like the tabloids because they concentrate on the seven deadly sins. These are weaknesses that all humans experience ... which, in turn, means that your stories will resonate with your audience. There is more about this in a later chapter.

In addition to the seven deadly sins we have the hierarchy of needs that Maslow suggests. These too can spark that creative idea that becomes a bestseller. They include the need for survival (food, drink, shelter, sleep), the need for safety (predictable environment, no anxiety), the need for love and belonging (affection from family, from friends, and from the group), the need for esteem (self-confidence, recognition, appreciation), and the need for self-actualisation (fulfilling one's potential). Again, these are factors that all human beings experience. Your audience can relate to them. The tabloids will have stories that revolve around these needs. All we have to do is to turn the events into the formula.

We will visit Maslow's hierarchy of needs in a later chapter.

People's Conversations

I know I shouldn't, but I do. I listen to other people's conversations. On the bus, on the train, on the Tube ... it doesn't matter. Well, they are public places. I watch out for phrases like, 'You wouldn't believe it, but ...' or, 'Do you know what he did ...?' or, 'She told him to get lost because ...' You've heard the phrases. You know you want to find out more. These are the titbits that can spark your top-selling story. Put what you hear into one of the formulas, use the seven deadly sins or Maslow's needs, and you are on your way to producing the epic we are all waiting for. Sometimes just listening to the conversation of others can give you a story even you wouldn't believe. But it got your attention. Pop it into the formula … and you may produce a bestseller.

The Work Environment

For people in employment the work scene is a hotbed of activity. Barely a day begins before it generates all sorts of tittle-tattle. 'We all went to the pub last night. You'll never guess who he left with …' Managers are a beloved target. 'She said she wanted to see me. Do you know what she said …?' 'She's only been here five minutes. I'll show her …' We all know exactly what you mean. Your audience does, too. That's why these episodes are a great source of audience interest. And why your audience loves you because you say what they are thinking. Pop it into the formula … and you have a story they'll love.

Other Stories

There is no copyright on ideas. Magazines, films, TV shows, and radio plays are all fodder for the brain. So if you want to write a story about an alien galaxy that wants to destroy the earth you are at liberty to do so. Or a murderer who wants to kill a prince. Or a scientist who wants to produce robotic humans. These stories have all been recorded. But your interpretation of events gives them a new flavour. Put your spin on an already successful story and you could be the next multimillionaire. Just check that the existing story follows one of the top-grossing formulas.

The examples section of the formula is where the story generates audience interest. BAD must do a few things that GOOD opposes. We all want to know what happened. GOOD must do a few things that BAD tries to stop. We all want to know what happened. The more examples of this conflict, the more your BAD/GOOD character will come across as determined to achieve their goal. And the greater the pull will be on your audience to view/read more.

You are the person who dictates the tone and pace of your story. You have a plethora of sources that provide stories where BAD dominates. You have a formula that you know generates top-grossing films/books. Use your resources and the formula. The world awaits your story.

CHAPTER 6
Some examples of quick, basic stories

I am going to use one of the tabloids to search for an idea that may generate a story. I am looking for a story that has the potential for:

- The evil character (BAD) does (action) something (goal) to harm the good character (GOOD).
- Deep down there is a reason (motivation) why BAD does this.
- The good character (GOOD) reacts and wants to defeat BAD.
- GOOD is involved in many mini episodes that may or may not relate to the ultimate goal.
- Each GOOD mini episode has its own goal, motivation, and actions.
- GOOD finally wins.

Here goes:
HERO PILOT SHOT DEAD.
A British helicopter pilot was shot down and killed by poachers he was following after they slaughtered three elephants. The pilot was helping rangers tackle Tanzania's illegal ivory trade when one of the gang blasted his chopper with an AK-47 assault rifle. The pilot managed to land in a game reserve after a bullet him in the leg ...

For me this paragraph met all the criteria of the top-grossing formula. Yes, I would have to tweak it. But I had a start, and this can be the hardest part of the creative process.

Let's work through the formula using details in this paragraph.

BAD is the poachers who want to stop the pilot from interfering by killing him.
BAD wants to get rich by selling ivory.
GOOD wants to stop the poachers and follows them.
(Possible mini episodes)

- GOOD meets woman who shares his views and they become lovers.
- GOOD spots poachers and radios police but poachers escape.
- GOOD runs out of fuel and almost crashes before reaching safety of airport.
- GOOD shot down by poachers but escapes to call the police.
- GOOD and police surround BAD and capture them.

The end.

CLIFF FALL KILLS SCHOOL TRIP LAD.
A boy of sixteen was found dead at the foot of a 120-foot cliff after going missing on a geography field trip. His body was recovered by coastguards after teachers reported him missing. The head described the boy as a keen sportsman who had the whole world ahead of him.

This one lends itself to variations. We could have the teachers as BAD. They raise these questions:

- Why didn't they know he was missing immediately?
- Were they drunk?
- Were they having an affair and forgot about the students?

We could have another sportsman as the culprit. The two boys could be rival contenders for the title of captain of the school team, perhaps. Could it be jealousy of the dead student's continual academic prowess? Could it be a bank robber who hid the cash in a cave in the mountain and the student found it?

The bank robber seems to have the most potential for now. Here goes:

BAD is the bank robber who wants to stop the student from finding the booty by killing him.
BAD wants to be rich.
GOOD wants to stop the robber and return the cash.
(Possible mini episodes)
- GOOD impresses his pals by climbing a dangerous cliff face and almost falls.
- GOOD enters cave. Sees cash, then robber. Escapes.
- GOOD tries to phone for police but battery dying. Robber almost catches him. Escapes.
- GOOD convinces other students to help him.
- GOOD and friends capture BAD. Police arrive and the school gets a reward for cash.
The end.

You probably noticed that I like a happy ending. You can tweak the original story to suit your epic. If you like happy endings … great. If you like a sad ending, so be it. You'll find both happy and sad endings in all top-grossing films and books.

OUR PAIN AT PIANO STAR WIFE.
The family of a world-renowned concert pianist yesterday told of their pain as her husband was found guilty of murdering her.

35

She was beaten then strangled to death on their second wedding anniversary. She had seventy-six injuries, had suffered repeated blows to the face, and her jawbone was snapped in half. The husband was a player of the double bass, who left his wife and two children in Norway to live with her in England.

These stories just keep coming. They're everywhere. You just have to look, and bear the formula in mind. Let's try this one:

BAD is the husband who wants to stop his wife from outshining him by killing her.
BAD is jealous.
GOOD wants to maintain her international reputation.
(Possible mini episodes)
- GOOD buys good piano but husband smashes it.
- GOOD flies to America to continue her career, but he follows and searches for her.
- GOOD plays at a major concert venue where husband tries to assassinate her.
- GOOD is wounded but not hurt.
- GOOD becomes even more famous and husband is put in prison for attempted murder.

The end.

The intention in this chapter is just to get something down on paper. You are not going to be brilliant at this stage. But you will create a possible outline, which you can develop later. You will get a feeling that this outline could develop into something spectacular.

You have probably noticed also that all my stories are about reality and not fantasy. You found in the research that four out of five films and books were about fantasy, not reality. But it does not take too much altering to convert your basic story into fantasy.

The *HERO PILOT SHOT DEAD* outline lends itself to an *Avatar*-type development. The helicopter could become the spaceship that scours the universe for illegal planet poachers. The pilot then beams down to tackle the poachers and defeats them.

The *CLIFF FALL KILLS SCHOOL TRIP LAD* outline could be reminiscent of Frodo having to climb to the top of the mountain to rid the world of evil. The cash could be the Philosopher's Stone from Harry Potter. The bank robber could be the evil Voldemort. The student falls down the mighty mountain only to be saved by an overhanging branch. He then climbs up and battles with the evil one, who falls to his death. The world is saved.

Just let your imagination run riot, and you could end up writing the story that could make you rich.

CREATE THE BEGINNING

CHAPTER 7
Now that you've finished – let's begin

In this chapter you will create an introduction. You will learn why the introduction is written after the text is finished.

To be creative your imagination needs to be allowed to run riot. You need to be free to decide how the BAD is trying to succeed (motive + goals + action).

Once you make the decision, the introduction to your story becomes easier. You can create a set-up that explains why (motive) the BAD wants to achieve its goal. Sometimes you can just imply the motive for the action and the reaction.

Star Wars: The Force Awakens is a good example. The formula tells us that the BAD character (First Order) has started to attack other planets once again. Not much is said about the GOOD character in relation to the BAD character. Nothing is said as to why the First Order has resumed its attacks.

Your audience wants to know why the GOOD character is motivated to defeat the BAD character. It wants to know what the situation is before the GOOD character gets involved. Your audience wants to know what's in it for the GOOD character if they succeed.

Conversely, your audience wants to know why the BAD character is motivated to defeat the GOOD character. It wants to know what the situation was before the GOOD character got involved. Your audience wants to know what's in it for the BAD character if they succeed.

Only characters who are totally obsessed with their goal and are determined to achieve it through action will interest your public. The issue for your main characters must become a do-or-die project. And total commitment is what your audience craves. The more committed your characters are to achieving their goal the more interest you generate in your audience.

In this chapter you will learn how to create an introduction and why an introduction is needed.

If we start with examples of an introduction you should start to see its value.
As a reminder, the BAD initiates the action.
Also, remember that the BAD can be a person, a place, a thing, an animal, a vegetable, or a mineral.

Let's start with top-grossing films.

Avatar
A greedy corporation, which uses an army colonel, wants to drive off the native Na'vi tribe from their native planet in order to mine the precious material in their land.

From this short summary you learn that
- The BAD is a person.
- BAD's motive is greed.
- BAD's goal is the precious material.
- BAD's action is to remove the Na'vi.

The GOOD is the Na'vi plus Jake.

- GOOD's motive is the love of their homeland.
- GOOD's goal is to save their homeland.
- GOOD's actions are to fight the colonel's attacks.
- GOOD wins when their planet is saved.

Harry Potter and the Philosopher's Stone
Lord Voldemort is the most evil dark wizard of all time. He wants to be all-powerful. Only Harry can stop him. He murders Harry Potter's parents but is unable to kill their son Harry. (After many episodes) Harry is destined to slay the evil Lord Voldemort and prevent him from being invincible.

From this synopsis you learn that the BAD is a spirit.
- BAD's motive is power.
- BAD's goal is to eliminate Harry.
- BAD's action is to kill Harry.

The GOOD is Harry Potter.
- GOOD's motive is to ensure peace for all.
- GOOD's goal is to defeat Voldemort.
- GOOD's actions lead to the defeat of Voldemort.
- GOOD wins when Lord Voldemort is destroyed.

Star Wars: The Force Awakens
The story begins thirty years after the events of Star Wars: Episode VI – Return of the Jedi. Luke Skywalker has vanished. In his absence the sinister First Order has risen from the ashes of the Galactic Empire and will not rest until Luke Skywalker, the last of the Jedi, has been destroyed along with the Republic. General Leia Organa is desperate to find her brother, Luke, in order to gain his help to restore peace to the

Galactic Empire. She leads the Resistance to attack the First Order.

From this paragraph, you learn that the BAD is a person.
- BAD's motivation is power.
- BAD's goal is to rule the universe.
- BAD's actions are to kill any opposition.

The GOOD is the Resistance.
- GOOD's motivation is to free the universe.
- GOOD's goal is to defeat the First Order.
- GOOD's actions are to fight the First Order.
- GOOD wins when the First Order is destroyed.

Let's now turn to the top-grossing books.

Remember, the lead is taken by the BAD element and BAD initiates the action.

The Lord of the Rings
Twenty rings existed. Three for elves, seven for dwarves, nine for humans and one made by the dark lord, Sauron, in Mordor, which would rule all the rings. Lord Sauron poured all his evil and all his will to dominate into his ring. An alliance of elves and humans resisted Lord Sauron's ring and fought against Mordor. Eventually, they won the battle and the ring fell to Isildur, who was the son of the King of Gondor. Just as Isildur was about to destroy the ring in Mount Doom, he changed his mind and held on to it for himself. Later he was killed and the ring fell to the bottom of the sea. The creature Gollum finds the ring and brings it to his cave. He then loses it to the hobbit Bilbo. The good wizard Gandalf realises the ring is the evil

Lord Sauron's ring. He wants Bilbo's nephew, Frodo, to go to Mount Doom and destroy it.

From this synopsis, you learn that the BAD is a supernatural being.
- BAD's motivation is power.
- BAD's goal is to rule the universe.
- BAD's actions are to kill any opposition.

The GOOD is Frodo.
- GOOD's motivation is to free the universe.
- GOOD's goal is to defeat Lord Sauron.
- GOOD's actions are to destroy the ring.
- GOOD wins when the ring is destroyed.

The Hobbit
The good wizard Gandalf persuading Bilbo to join a group of dwarves to reclaim their treasure and the Lonely Mountain from the dragon Smaug.

From this summary, you learn that the BAD is a dragon.
From this introduction, we learn that the BAD is a person.
- BAD's motivation is power.
- BAD's goal is to keep all the gold.
- BAD's actions are to kill an opposition.

The GOOD is Bilbo.
- GOOD's motivation is to return the homeland to the dwarves.
- GOOD's goal is to defeat the dragon.
- GOOD's actions are to fight the dragon.
- GOOD wins when the dragon is destroyed.

And Then There Were None
Eight people are puzzled as to why they have been invited to a mansion on an island. They assemble for dinner. They hear a recorded voice that accuses each of them of a specific murder that was committed in the past but was never uncovered. One by one, the voice (U.N. Owen) murders them. The guests search for the voice to save themselves.

From this paragraph, you learn that the BAD is a person.
- BAD's motivation is justice.
- BAD's goal is to kill people who escaped justice.
- BAD's actions are to kill the guilty people.

The GOOD are the victims.
- GOOD's motivation is to save their lives.
- GOOD's goal is to defeat the killer.
- GOOD's actions are to fight the killer.
- GOOD wins when the killer is destroyed.

The introduction helps the viewer/reader to understand why BAD/GOOD wants its goal. It may be a GOOD goal or a BAD goal. But we understand why the BAD/GOOD character wants it. There is the motive: a driving force that propels the character to action. The motive may be power, justice, or greed.

The introduction also introduces the audience to the terminology that they will encounter.
Are you setting the scene in a future galaxy or on a remote island? Are you talking human beings or elves? Your audience

is very willing to suspend belief so long as they know the BAD/GOOD element and its motives.

The introduction is the way you get the audience to switch from their way of thinking to your way of thinking.

The introduction helps your audience to guess what could happen next, and you give them avenues that could lead to the solution.

In summary, this chapter deals with the beginning of a story. Your audience/reader wants to know that the BAD element is taking the initiative and the GOOD element is reacting. Your introduction sets the stage, the expected vocabulary, the expected costumes, the expected objects, the expected terrain, the expected motives, and the expected actions.

In your introduction you move your audience/reader into your world.

YOU'VE GOT THE BASICS – NOW ELABORATE:

CHARACTERS
MOTIVES + GOALS + ACTIONS

CHAPTER 8
Characters: bad and good

Your aim in the first few chapters was to learn what makes a good story and how to create a basic one very quickly. You now have the basic formula to do this. You know where to find ideas, and you can create a simple story quickly and easily.

In the next few chapters you will take that basic story and embellish it.

In this chapter you will learn that there are many representations of BAD. Once you have selected your BAD this will colour your story. It will dictate the time, the place, the costumes, and the gadgets that your audience will experience.

BAD

A BAD is a being that everyone believes to be evil.

But BAD can have many interpretations. This is a mindset that you may need to work on. You need to understand that BAD can be a human, an alien, an animal, or nature itself.

BAD could be a manager who prevents you from advancing your career. It could be a doctor who sees you as a source of organs. Even a traffic warden who gleefully issues a parking ticket can be seen as a bad character. It could be a maniacal mad professor who wants to bomb a country and dominate the world.

BAD could be a ghost who seeks to terrorise us. It could be an alien that is determined to destroy the human race. It could be a being with supernatural powers who wants to exterminate humans.

BAD could be a bear, a raging bull, or an angry ape. BAD could be seagulls or bees or snakes. Even a household pet could turn on people.

BAD could be a tsunami, a gale, or a thunderstorm. It could be a river that floods and damages homes. It could be the heat of the desert or the freezing cold of the Antarctic.

BAD is all around us. It can inspire a story. Your creativity will provide the examples and the story.

Remember, the BAD being initiates the action. Knowing what the BAD is has many advantages for you:

You can establish the time and place of this story.
By establishing that the First Order is an interplanetary being in *Star Wars: The Force Awakens* you immediately prepare your audience for spaceships, aliens, planets, and galactic battles.

You can introduce the qualities of both BAD and GOOD.
In *Harry Potter and the Philosopher's Stone* the BAD is continually trying to kill Harry (the GOOD), while Harry shows many examples of him rescuing his companions.

You can remind your audience of the ultimate goal.

In *The Lord of the Rings* there are many instances where the ring exerts an evil influence on the GOOD, which reinforces the need to destroy the ring to remove its power.

While the BAD has many traits, so does the GOOD. While it is the BAD that takes the lead, the GOOD is involved in mini episodes which need some indication of its basic characteristics. This heightens the tension between the BAD and GOOD and maintains the attention of your audience.

GOOD

The GOOD is a being that everyone believes to be kind and generous and which strives for freedom for all.

But GOOD can have many interpretations. GOOD also can be human, alien, animal, or nature.

GOOD could be a doctor who does research to find a cure for the terrible disease. A traffic warden who turns a blind eye to a parking offence is a contender for a GOOD character. A soldier who lies on a bomb to protect the innocent could be another contender.

GOOD can be a supernatural force that helps humans. It could be a fairy godmother, an elf, a human with super powers, or even a wizard.

GOOD can be a guide dog, a rabbit that talks, or a cat that comforts. It can be a bear that dances or an elephant that rescues.

GOOD can be rain in the desert or shade from the heat. It can be food for the starving or water for the thirsty.

GOOD characters are all around us. They can inspire a story. Your creativity will provide the examples and the story.

In summary, BAD and GOOD form the basis of a great story. The function of both BAD and GOOD must be established early, and with conviction. The filmgoer or reader must be in no doubt as to which being is BAD and which being is GOOD. This is an element of a successful story.

CHAPTER 9
Characters: are you air, fire, water, or earth?

In the following chapters about a character you will find numerous traits that you can use to flesh out your BAD and your GOOD. You may find that a certain characteristic triggers a creative idea. The more original your story the closer you are to producing a top-grossing story.

Once you have your character, BAD or GOOD, you may want to give them qualities and physical descriptions that make them more evil or more virtuous. Remember, in all five top-grossing films and books the BAD and the GOOD had human characteristics, regardless of their physical appearance.

The Greeks grouped people into four categories, and found they had identifiable qualities. Greek physicians were very aware that there were different types of people. Bit by bit they grouped their patients into four categories. When they were ill each group had the same symptoms. Each group was given the same medicine. It seemed to cure them. The four categories are fire, air, earth, and water. So which category are you?

The Four Elements

FIRE
Here are some of the qualities of the fire temperament:
- Short
- Compact
- Energetic
- Strong opinions

- Leadership
- Generous
- If crossed, have bad tempers
- Associated with the colour red.

AIR
Here are some of the qualities of the air temperament:
- Tall and thin
- Full of nervous energy
- Always on the move
- Often with lighter-coloured hair and paler skin
- Sociable
- Fun to be with
- Full of new ideas
- Short attention spans
- Lack concentration
- Associated with the colour yellow.

EARTH
Here are some of the qualities of the earth temperament:
- Tall and thin
- Deep-set eyes
- Sensitive
- Find the world a difficult place to live in
- Feel misunderstood
- Inflexible
- Daring
- Empathetic
- Associated with the colour blue.

WATER
Here are some of the qualities of the water temperament:
- Overweight

- Slow
- Have a calming presence
- Great in a crisis
- No sense of urgency
- Associated with the colour green.

Could you use any of these qualities or physical descriptions to give more depth to your characters both BAD and GOOD?

Again, you should remember that all top-grossing films and books have beings that have human characteristics. Whether they are human, supernatural, animal, or nature, they probably have some of these features.

The Four Elements and the Zodiac Signs

Each zodiac sign is said to be ruled by the four elements. Have a look at the combination of traits associated with the four elements in terms of their corresponding zodiac sign.

Earth: (Taurus, Virgo, Capricorn)
Those with earth sign influence are:

- Well-grounded and down-to-earth types.
- Hard workers who will get the job done.
- Not risk-takers and prefer a steady, stable path.
- Reliable, dutiful, conservative, logical, and responsible.
- Appreciate all that can be seen and touched.
- Like to accumulate worldly possessions.
- Love the finer things in life and will strive to situate themselves accordingly.
- May become greedy and too materialistic.

- Step upon others to gratify themselves.

Air: (Gemini, Libra, Aquarius)
Those with air sign influence are:

- Smart and enterprising.
- Love a puzzle or dilemma and will find unique solutions.
- Inventive and think out of the box.
- Generally optimistic and tend to think of the glass as half full.
- Thrive on processing information and are curious and alert.
- Can be cold and calculating, not fully understanding the emotional needs of others.

Fire: (Aries, Leo, Sagittarius)
Those with fire sign influence are:

- Self-sufficient, courageous risk-takers.
- Go at life with gusto, including in their relationships.
- Are by far the sexiest of the elemental signs.
- Are fun, engaging, and creative in all aspects of their lives.
- Can be terribly selfish, demanding, and boss under unfavourable conditions.
- Often refuse to see any side but their own when confronted with an issue.
- Can be very headstrong, and will bully their way through life if life doesn't move over for them.

Water: (Cancer, Scorpio, Pisces)

Those with water sign influence are:

- The feelers of the world.
- Intuitive, and 'just know'.
- Compassionate and receptive, and feel everything quite deeply.
- Artistic, and love having beauty around them.
- Form strong emotional bonds with others.
- Are always willing to help.
- Want to care for others and be cared for.
- Are the psychics of the world.
- Can be moody, and may tend to dwell on the bad things.

The beings in your stories may need some characteristics that are human: traits that your audience can relate to. These lists give you some ideas as to how to humanise your characters.

CHAPTER 10
Characters: horoscope

You have considered the qualities of a character in the categories of Air, Fire, Water, and Earth. Consider now only the specific zodiac sign of a character. Each month in the zodiac creates a being with distinctive qualities. You could include some of these qualities in your description of a character.

AQUARIUS: TRAITS

Strengths: Progressive, original, independent, humanitarian.
Weaknesses: Runs from emotional expression, temperamental, uncompromising, aloof.
Aquarius likes: Fun with friends, helping others, fighting for causes, intellectual conversation, good listeners.
Aquarius dislikes: Limitations, broken promises, being lonely, dull or boring situations, people who disagree with them.

Aquarius (January 20–February 18):
Aquarians are extremely vulnerable and sensitive. Although you may often find them being surrounded by many friends they rarely have close friends and in reality. Aquarius is a universal sign, which makes them public people. Hence, Aquarians are often associated with clubs, organisations, and forums, and enthusiastically participate in intellectual discussions. Aquarians are great communicators as long as they are within their mental realm.

PISCES: TRAITS

Strengths: Compassionate, artistic, intuitive, gentle, wise, musical.

Weaknesses: Fearful, overly trusting, sad, desire to escape reality, can be a victim or a martyr.

Pisces likes: Being alone, sleeping, music, romance, visual media, swimming, spiritual themes.

Pisces dislikes: Know-it-all, being criticised, the past coming back to haunt them, cruelty of any kind.

Pisces (February 19–March 20):
Pisceans live in their imaginary world, which barely has a connection with reality. They love to look at the world through a rosy window. When challenged by reality Pisceans have the tendency to retreat into their world of imagination.

ARIES: TRAITS

Strengths: Courageous, determined, confident, enthusiastic, optimistic, honest, passionate.

Weaknesses: Impatient, moody, short-tempered, impulsive, aggressive.

Aries likes: Comfortable clothes, taking on leadership roles, physical challenges, individual sports.

Aries dislikes: Inactivity, delays, work that does not use one's talents.

Aries (March 21–April 19):
Aries demonstrate a strong personality. They have strong leadership qualities and are honest and straightforward. Aries

often have strong determination and can't be deterred by failures. Aries are always eager for action. They take up leadership spontaneously but they don't judge the pros and cons of a situation before acting. This also makes them vulnerable.

TAURUS: TRAITS

Strengths: Reliable, patient, practical, devoted, responsible, stable.
Weaknesses: Stubborn, possessive, uncompromising.
Taurus likes: Gardening, cooking, music, romance, high-quality clothes, working with hands.
Taurus dislikes: Sudden changes, complications, insecurity of any kind, synthetic fabric.

Taurus (April 20–May 20):
Taureans are noted for their determination and zeal. It is not easy to distract a Taurean from his goal once he has set his target. He would stay focused on his target and would continuously strive to achieve it. Taureans attach high value to simplicity and functionality. They often live a life that is simple and devoid of luxury.

GEMINI: TRAITS

Strengths: Gentle, affectionate, curious, adaptable, ability to learn quickly and to exchange ideas.
Weaknesses: Nervous, inconsistent, indecisive.
Gemini likes: Music, books, magazines, chats with nearly everyone, short trips around the town.

Gemini dislikes: Being alone, being confined, repetition, and routine.

Gemini (May 21–June 20):
Geminis are full of duality. They always look at a situation from a dual perspective. Geminis are characterised by inconstancy and a dual nature. Geminis, therefore, always stay confused about their feelings. Geminis, however, are strong communicators and express good control over language. They are often found to have the knowledge of several languages.

CANCER: TRAITS

Strengths: Tenacious, highly imaginative, loyal, emotional, sympathetic, persuasive.
Weaknesses: Moody, pessimistic, suspicious, manipulative, insecure.
Cancer likes: Art, home-based hobbies, relaxing near or in water, helping loved ones, a good meal with friends.
Cancer dislikes: Strangers, any criticism of Mum, revealing their personal life.

Cancer (June 21–July 22):
Cancerians are emotional. Their lives are often affected by mood shifts. You can find a Cancerian in several different moods even over the course of a single day. The true emotion of Cancer, however, is hidden behind their composure … but they are soft creatures, and can be hurt easily by unkind words. People of the Cancer zodiac sign can be prone to depression and other mental issues. However, Cancerians are great family people and enjoy big families around them.

LEO: TRAITS

Strengths: Creative, passionate, generous, warm-hearted, cheerful, humorous.
Weaknesses: Arrogant, stubborn, self-centred, lazy, inflexible.
Leo likes: Theatre, taking holidays, being admired, expensive things, bright colours, fun with friends.
Leo dislikes: Being ignored, facing difficult realities, not being treated like a king or a queen.

Leo (July 23–August 22):
Leos are warm-spirited. They are full of energy, and always eager to jump into action. Leos crave recognition and admiration. Leos always love to be at the centre of attraction. They strive to reach the top in whatever they do. Leos always love to be surrounded by large crowds and admirers. However, they do not often take kindly to criticism and take the words of critics to heart. Leos are very ambitious, and choose their acquaintances carefully. They aspire to higher social recognition.

VIRGO: TRAITS

Strengths: Loyal, analytical, kind, hard-working, practical.
Weaknesses: Shyness, worry, overly critical of self and others, all work and no play.
Virgo likes: Animals, healthy food, books, nature, cleanliness.
Virgo dislikes: Rudeness, asking for help, taking centre stage.

Virgo (August 23–September 22):
Virgos have a keen sense of good and bad in that they are highly discriminating. Their intuition leads them to identify the wrong motives in people. Hence, Virgos exercise extreme

caution in what they do. The virgin represents purity, and therefore they are endowed with the ability to distinguish the good from the bad. Hence, Virgos are also cleanliness freaks. Despite their intelligence Virgos often remain confused about the decisions they make in their life. Also, you will not find Virgos in a hive of activity.

LIBRA: TRAITS

Strengths: Co-operative, diplomatic, gracious, fair-minded, sociable.

Weaknesses: Indecisive, avoids confrontations, will carry a grudge, self-pity.

Libra likes: Harmony, gentleness, sharing with others, the outdoors.

Libra dislikes: Violence, injustice, loudmouths, conformity.

Libra (September 23–October 22):
Libra is an active sign, and members born under the sign are endowed with high energy. But Librans also tend to run out of their energy quickly. The Libra sign is the balancing sign, and people born under this sign have a very balanced mind. They can be often found in settling disputes. Librans always try to maintain harmony and balance. They are also very level-headed and have a keen sense of justice. Their suggestions are therefore often highly sought after by their friends and kinsmen. Librans are two-faceted characters. They have both cheerfulness and darkness in them. Librans have phases of heightened activities but they can easily slip into phases of complete inactivity and apathy as well.

SCORPIO: TRAITS

Strengths: Resourceful, brave, passionate, stubborn, a true friend.

Weaknesses: Distrusting, jealous, secretive, violent.

Scorpio likes: Truth, facts, being right, long-time friends, teasing, a grand passion.

Scorpio dislikes: Dishonesty, revealing secrets, passive people.

Scorpio (October 23–November 21):
Scorpios are the most diverse in nature and therefore present the most interesting study. Scorpios hold a grudge, and would wait patiently for the right moment to strike. They are not likely to forget any act of betrayal or treachery. For Scorpios what is implied is more fascinating than the obvious. Scorpios are often described as egoists. However, some of the positive traits of Scorpios are diplomacy, intuition, intelligence, being engaging, resolute, spirituality, and sensitivity.

SAGITTARIUS: TRAITS

Strengths: Generous, idealistic, great sense of humour.

Weaknesses: Promises more than can deliver, very impatient, will say anything no matter how undiplomatic.

Sagittarius likes: Freedom, travel, philosophy, being outdoors.

Sagittarius dislikes: Clingy people, being constrained, off-the-wall theories, details.

Sagittarius (November 22–December 21):
Sagittarians are the incurable optimists. They are always looking at the positive side of a thing. Their optimism can't be dampened by hardships or negative results. Sagittarians are often outdoor types. They will take an interest in all sorts of

sports and outdoor activities. They are also adventurous in nature. Although they are true to a fault they can also turn completely deaf to criticism and turn down suggestions.

CAPRICORN: TRAITS

Strengths: Responsible, disciplined, self-control, good managers.
Weaknesses: Know-it-all, unforgiving, condescending, expecting the worst.
Capricorn likes: Family, tradition, music, understated status, quality craftsmanship
Capricorn dislikes: Almost everything at some point.

Capricorn (December 22–January 19):
Members of this sign have an insatiable desire to climb higher and, while following this path, they can also become selfish and might not hesitate to sacrifice the interests of others in fulfilling their goals. Capricorns may seem risk-averse, but in reality they carefully plan all their moves ahead and rehearse them to perfection.

You now have a selection of qualities that your characters, BAD or GOOD, could have to give them both a third dimension and human qualities.

CHAPTER 11

Motivation: goals and action

Having dealt with the many interpretations and several of the qualities of the BAD and the GOOD you now need to look at the reason why these characters act and react. In this chapter you will be adding motivation, goals, and actions to your arsenal of writing tools.

Psychologists are pretty unanimous in their belief that everybody does something for a reason, no matter how hidden the explanation may be. Indeed, strong characters must have a good reason to act if they are to overcome the obstacles before they achieve their goal.

There have been lots definitions of motivation but a common theme is that motivation is a force that energises, activates, and directs behaviour. Motivation is what makes us act the way we do. Motives arise from a desire to accomplish a goal. Motivation is general and internal. Goals are more specific and tangible. And actions are the way motives turn into goals.

A being that is motivated will act in a certain way. This presumes that a goal exists. It assumes there will be action.

Motivation involves goals and action.

In this chapter you will see an ingredient that is common to all top-grossing films and books. Characters in top-grossing films and books are motivated to achieve a goal by action.

In all the top-grossing films and books the main characters are motivated to achieve their goals, which is usually something physical (the 'what'). It is their life-or-death determination to succeed in achieving this goal that makes these stories so compelling.

But the 'what' is always preceded by a 'why', which is a mental state, a decision, or something that cannot be seen. People do not just want something or to do something. They want something 'because'. They do something 'because'. The 'why' always precedes the 'what'. Knowing 'why' and 'what' helps to explain people's actions. That is why the 'why' (the motivation) is needed to explain the character's goal. The action provides the 'how' of the character's motivation to achieve their goal.

BAD: motivation, goals, and action

In *Avatar* the colonel is a soldier who prides himself on always completing his mission (motivation = why). He will defeat the Na'vi (goal = what) by killing them all (action = how).
Jake loves the Na'vi people (motivation = why). He is determined to save them (goal = what) and will fight to protect them (action = how).

In *Titanic* Caledon Hockley feels insignificant (motivation = why). He wants everyone to worship him (goal = what). He will humiliate anyone who does not worship him (action = how).

In *Star Wars: The Force Awakens* the First Order wants to be all-powerful (motivation = why). It wants all creatures to bow before it (goal = why) and will destroy everything that opposes it (action = how).

In *The Avengers Assemble* Loki wants to be all-powerful (motivation = why). He is determined to get the elixir of life (goal = what) and will kill anyone who stops him getting it (action = how).

In *And Then There Were None* we see the voice seeking justice (motivation = why) by killing all those who deserve death (goal = what). He uses different methods to kill the victims (action = how).

Without exception, all the top-grossing films and books have BAD with one motive. They also have BAD with one goal, which initiates the actions to achieve that goal.

GOOD: motivation, goals, and action

Now we will look at the GOOD and their many motivations, many goals, and many actions.

The GOOD needs more explanation. It differs from the BAD in that there can be many motivations, many goals, and many actions. The specific goals and actions may not necessarily be related to the immediate goal.

GOOD can be involved in mini episodes that do not relate to their goal.

Jake, in *Avatar*, at first supports the colonel and spies on the Na'vi. Then he is attacked by wild beasts and is rescued. Then he falls in love with the Na'vi woman and strives to defeat the colonel.

Harry Potter and the Philosopher's Stone shows Harry winning the game of Quidditch, then fooling the three dogs that guard the cellar.

Titanic has Rose in the suicide incident one moment, and then braving the waters to rescue Jack in the next.

Ley in *Star Wars: The Force Awakens* fights alien creatures for scrap metal in one scene, then battles the First Order in another.

In *Jurassic World* Aunt Claire is in a confrontation with her sister in one scene, and in the next she is involved in an episode where she has to escape death from the dinosaur's bite.

And Then There Were None reveals the good characters trying to find the murderer in many different ways, but not succeeding in doing so.

This variation of scenes where the GOOD has to struggle with a variety of mini BADs is found in all the top-grossing films and books.

In summary, the BAD has one major goal throughout the story. All the scenarios involving the BAD are related to that one goal. However, the GOOD has many goals and is the subject of many scenarios involving mini BADs.
However, the GOOD always survives, and each scenario tells us how the GOOD survives.

CHAPTER 12

Motivation: the seven deadly sins

In the previous chapter you learnt how people have a reason (motivation = why) for attaining something (goals = what) by any means (action = how). You saw examples of this in a selection of top-grossing films and books.

In this chapter you will be introduced to more motives (why) that explain BAD's behaviour and GOOD's behaviour (action = how).

You will also find the answer to the question, "What can I write about that will interest lots and lots of viewers or readers?"

The answer is to find the qualities that BAD characters cannot control. Alternatively, you could find the qualities that GOOD characters can control. Either way you are tapping into the psyche of every human being, which is great for getting the attention of your audience. It also explains why your character is acting in a certain way throughout your story.

THE SEVEN DEADLY SINS

As early as 387 AD a monk called Evagrius Ponticus looked at humanity, and thought deeply. He asked, "What concerns all human beings?" He discovered the answer could be summarised in the seven deadly sins. Evagrius Ponticus noted that the seven deadly sins could be a source of weakness or a source of strength. Your story will follow the BAD character acting then the GOOD character reacting.

As a writer, knowing the seven deadly sins will enable you to relate to a global audience. The seven deadly sins are:

- Pride
- Envy
- Greed
- Gluttony
- Lust
- Anger
- Sloth.

(Or PEG GLAS, if you are into mnemonics.)

PRIDE
One definition of pride includes:
'Vanity, excessive love of self, magnifying the defects of others.'

But there are many more interpretations. If you google 'pride' you will discover that pride can include:
- A desire to be important.
- Wanting to be attractive to others.
- Thinking you are better than you are.
- Thinking you are the source of your own greatness.
- Seeking attention and honour for yourself.
- Magnifying the defects of others.
- Hating your inferiors for fear they may equal you.
- Hating your superiors because they are above you.

ENVY

One definition of envy is:
'A feeling of discontented or resentful longing aroused by someone else's possessions, qualities, or luck; desire to have a quality, possession, or other desirable thing belonging to (someone else)'.

But there are many more interpretations. If you google 'envy' you will discover that envy can include:
- Jealousy.
- Hating others for what they have.
- Thinking you should have more even though others have less.
- Resenting the good that others receive.
- Resentment of your neighbour.
- Feeling good when others suffer a setback.

GREED
One definition of greed is:
'Excessive consumption of or desire for food; excessive desire, as for wealth or power'.

But there are many more interpretations. If you google 'greed' you will discover that greed can include:
- Wanting more things than you need.
- Love of money.
- Love of power.
- A selfish desire for more of something.
- Taking from those in need.
- Using people to gain an advantage.

GLUTTONY
One definition of gluttony is:

'Excess in eating or drinking. Greedy or excessive indulgence'.

But there are many more interpretations. If you google 'gluttony' you will discover that gluttony can include:
- The inordinate desire to consume more than you require.
- Excessive consumption of something.
- Use of food or drink to injure your health.
- Use of food or drink to impair your mental faculties.

ANGER (WRATH)
One definition of anger is:
'A strong feeling of annoyance, displeasure, or hostility. To fill (someone) with anger; provoke anger in someone'.

But there are many more interpretations. If you google 'wrath', you will discover that wrath/anger can include:
- Verbal violence.
- Thoughts about desire for revenge.
- Wanting to hurt someone.
- Desire for vengeance.

SLOTH (LAZINESS)
One definition of sloth is:
'Reluctance to work or make an effort; laziness. Apathy. Dullness'.

But there are many more interpretations. If you google 'sloth', you will discover that sloth can include:
- Idleness.
- Wasting time.
- Avoidance of physical work.

- No desire to make sacrifices.
- Neglect of duties.
- Procrastination.
- Reluctance to cultivate a virtue.

LUST
One definition of lust is:
'Strong sexual desire. To have strong sexual desire for someone'.

But there are many more interpretations. If you google 'lust' you will discover that lust can include:
- Inordinate craving for pleasures of the body.
- Lust for money.
- Lust for power.
- Treating others as sex objects.
- Seeing others as bodies rather than people.

In summary, you now have the elements that are of interest to all audiences. These elements are the seven deadly sins.

The seven deadly sins form the basis of most of the tabloid press articles. The tabloid press sells millions. They fascinate lots of people. You want lots of people to be fascinated by your work. Use the seven deadly sins as motivators for your characters, and you could be writing a story that will make you rich.

CHAPTER 13

Motivation: the five needs

If the last chapter did not give you enough reasons for characters to act then this chapter might help.

Abraham Maslow was a psychologist who studied the needs that motivated people. He grouped these needs into five major categories. Each major category could be subdivided. The five major categories of needs are:

- SURVIVAL
- SAFETY
- LOVE AND BELONGING
- ESTEEM
- SELF-ACTUALISATION.

While the psychological identification of each need is not our primary concern, they provide a wonderful motive for writers. For the BAD they become a great way to punish the GOOD. For the GOOD they can provide an incentive for destroying the BAD or for overcoming minor challenges.

In the following paragraphs there is an explanation of each need and its positive use by the GOOD, or its negative use by the BAD.

SURVIVAL
- Food
- Drink
- Shelter

- Sleep
- Air.

The need for survival encompasses the physiological requirements. These include the need for food, drink, shelter, sleep, and air. They concern the body, and are the concerns of all beings. Animals need food: birds need food. These needs are very basic, and are shared by all creatures.

So how does this help us as writers? No matter who the character is, or what its social status, this being is controlled by these needs. For example, the person who is starving has no other interest but food. They dream of food, think about food, and want only food. All other needs are forgotten. Such is the power of the physiological needs.

The GOOD character can be motivated by the physiological needs.

The BAD character can use the physiological needs to punish the GOOD character.

SAFETY
- Predictable environment
- Feeling secure
- Structure
- Rules
- No economic anxiety
- No psychological anxiety.

The need for safety and security includes the need of freedom from physical, economic, or psychological worry. We want to live in a stable and predictable environment. We need structure with rules and laws to reduce chaos. A society that is peaceful and organised makes its members feel safe. The possibility of threats from wild animals, criminals, and murderers is greatly reduced. The threat of chaos and lack of predictability can produce a constraint in a character's ability to function.

For the GOOD character they may strengthen the motivation to succeed.

For the BAD character they are ways to humiliate the GOOD character.

LOVE AND BELONGING
- Connection with other people
- Affection
- Part of a family
- Part of a group
- Part of society.

All people need a love that involves giving and receiving affection. We hunger for a place in the group or in the family. The pangs of loneliness, rejection, and ostracism become dominant when this need is not met. There is a need for contact, intimacy, and a sense of belonging. We dread isolation, loneliness, and alienation.

For the GOOD character this may strengthen their determination to succeed.

For the BAD character they are ways to weaken and dominate the GOOD character.

ESTEEM
- Self-confidence
- Recognition
- Fame
- Being appreciated
- Being respected.

We all crave for a high evaluation of ourselves. We want respect. We want the admiration of others. We want prestige. We want status, fame, and glory. We want to be appreciated. Achieving self-esteem leads to feelings of self-confidence, of worth, and of adequacy. However, if we deny these needs we produce feelings of inferiority and weakness. This in turn gives rise to discouragement.

For the GOOD character lack of prestige may strengthen their determination to succeed.

For the BAD character they are ways to weaken the GOOD character and make them surrender.

SELF-ACTUALISATION
- Achieving one's potential.
- Accomplishing what we want in life.
- Discovering our purpose in life.
- Attaining the things we consider important.

The need for self-actualisation is regarded by Maslow as the highest pinnacle of human attainment. Self-actualisation is the individual doing what they feel destined for. A musician feels destined to play music. An artist feels destined to produce pictures. We all believe we have a special quality. We have that desire to actualise the gifts that we potentially have. We want to become everything that we are capable of becoming.

For the GOOD character self-actualisation may mean fulfilling the role they chose and love.

For the BAD character self-actualisation means accomplishing their evil goal or denying the GOOD character the opportunity to develop the qualities that they possess.

All beings in the top-grossing films and books are motivated to achieve a goal through action. You, as a writer, now have many motives to choose from. Each motive has a separate goal. You now have many goals to choose from. Achieving each goal requires action.

Now your task becomes not 'What will interest my audience?' but 'Which motive and goals, from the dozens available, will I choose for my story?' You are at the point where you have many options from which to choose instead of being frozen and suffering from writer's block. All the strands of your creative mind can now weave a spellbinding story that will hypnotise your audience.

STORYTELLING and the BRAIN

Chapter 14
What has death got to do with storytelling?

In previous chapters you were looking for the components of a top-grossing story. You analysed the five top-grossing stories in films and books and noted the common factors.

Two factors stood out immediately: death and evil. This chapter examines why death and evil are favoured by storytellers. Episodes that involve death and near death are magnets that draw your audience to your work (you will see why when we examine the brain in a later chapter).

Death is always associated with something evil. This is why evil (BAD) is found in the top-grossing films and books. This chapter explains why. As with BAD and with GOOD, there are many interpretations of death. Dying, near death, survival from death, murder, serious injury, and illness are all terms associated with death.

This chapter starts with an explanation of why death and survival are so important to all mankind. Talk about death and survival and your audience will pay attention. That is guaranteed.

For 500 million years creatures have been fighting to survive (and, at times, quite literally, fighting). Anything to do with survival immediately compels the attention of your audience. We are preprogrammed to respond to anything relating to survival. It's been happening for over 500 million years, so why should your audience change now? They won't.

Your audience is programmed to pay attention to situations that threaten survival – and not just survival of self but the survival of offspring. There are two types of survival: survival of self and survival of the species. By protecting and ensuring the life of the offspring the parent can ensure the survival of the species. Anything to do with the harming of offspring will attract the attention of the audience. The members of the audience are programmed to pay attention to the survival of offspring and the continuation of the species just as much as they are programmed to pay attention to the survival of self.

So ... the number one factor that will grab the attention of your audience is something to do with survival: survival of self or survival of offspring. And they can't help themselves: it's preprogrammed inside them.

Consider now the many ways that beings can experience a form of death or survive death:

Death to the body (organs)
Cancer, poison, hunger, thirst – they all grab the attention of the audience. Your audience has experienced these conditions, or they have friends who have experienced these pains. Your audience knows what you're talking about. You're talking about survival. And they can relate to your story.

Death to the body (senses)
(Hearing) loud noises, (sight) bright lights, fast movement ... they all grab the attention of the audience. Your audience knows that these experiences can signal danger. Millions of years ago they were in situations where they happened, and they needed a response if they were to survive.

Death from the environment (nature)

Floods, falling rocks, lightning, snakes – they are all factors that affect survival. Your audience has experienced or witnessed someone else experience these dangers. Your audience can relate to what you say in your story and will pay attention to environmental factors. It concerns survival.

Death from the environment (society)

Guns, war, knives, punches – they are obvious physical dangers. But there are other dangers that are less brutal – unemployment, poverty, homelessness, and arguments: social factors that ultimately affect our survival and cause pain. Your audience has experienced these social threats to survival or they know of someone who has. They will understand this element because we are all programmed to survive. And, in this case, survive in society.

Death of offspring (children)

We are programmed not only to ensure our own survival but also the survival of our children. We cannot help but protect not only our own lives but also the lives of our offspring, who will continue the species. We long for and protect offspring so that the species can survive. If there are no children to continue the species parents will go to great lengths to be blessed with a child.

Death of a partner (male-female relationship)

Related to our concerns for the survival of our children is a concern for the relationship with our partner. Without partners males and females cannot combine to produce offspring. This, in turn, means that the species will not survive. Consequently, any threat to the harmony of a relationship will create interest in your audience.

Does your story contain elements that relate to dangers to the body or from the environment or from society or to the death of offspring? These are all factors that everyone can relate to, and they will capture the attention of your audience.

Chapter 15
Other ways to get the attention of your audience

You have seen how death and survival will seize the attention of your audience, but how do you sustain it? How do you keep you viewers or readers on the edge of their seats? The following paragraphs will show you how the master storytellers maintained the interest of their audience.

Get the attention of the audience by showing another person in pain.

The audience will focus on your words when you relate situations where others felt pain. Part of the brain empathises with others. The brain of the audience feels their pain. Your audience knows that the other's pain could be their pain and a threat to their survival. They will pay attention to stories that involve pain.

Does your story contain situations where your main character experiences pain?

Describe actions and you will get their attention.

Part of our brain activates the motor regions. Scientists have found that when we witness others performing actions our motor regions are activated. When we see others fighting we feel ourselves throwing or receiving the punch. When we see others on the edge of a cliff we feel the same sensations as our character. Our audience cannot help themselves when they experience the actions of others. They respond. It is built into their brain.

Does your story include scenes where harmful action takes place?

We need love. This resonates with all audiences.

All creatures in a social setting have a want for and a need of affection. It is part of our make-up. We want to be loved. Our brain needs it. Our brain will not function normally in a social manner if we do not have affection. You will grab the attention of your audience if you mention characters who are not being loved. Your characters want to be loved. Your audience empathises. They feel the character's pain.

Does your story suggest that the main character receives no affection?

Rules: "You wouldn't believe what they just did." The audience loves this.

Modern society gets more and more complex. We have traditions from previous centuries, rules from our childhood, and guidance from our present-day mentors. "Do this ... do that". If we have to obey the rules then so should everyone else. Your audience knows the feeling when somebody breaks an accepted rule. It wakes them up. They pay attention. When someone breaks a rule your audience will feel anger or superiority. They will react. You have got their attention.

Did the evil character break any rules in your story?

Present a problem and your audience will be trying to solve it.

Mankind's supreme talent is the ability to hold one thought in the brain and simultaneously compare it with other thoughts. Your audience has that facility. When confronted with danger the brain has the ability to identify the danger and compare it with possible solutions and their outcomes, and then decide on a final solution. We have been doing this for a million years. We are good at it. So is your audience. Pose a problem and your audience is programmed to come up with possible solutions. They are fully attentive. They want to know if they are correct or not. They focus on your answer. You have their attention.

In summary, your audience will pay attention to factors that go back millions of years. We are a body-environment-brain creature, and these elements have left memories in each layer of the brain.

Know the factors that lead to survival, use them in your story, and you will have your audience in the palm of your hand. You will be a master storyteller.

Chapter 16

A quick tour of the brain, and why your audience will pay attention

In this chapter you will take a quick look at the brain. You will see how it developed over millions of years, and how it grew from a simple brainstem to a highly complex cortex that is capable of immense feats. More importantly, you will realise that you are not just a creature of the millennium but have roots dating back 500 million years.

Scientists have discovered that there are three distinct layers in the brain. The brainstem (dating back around 500 million years), the midbrain (dating back around 200 million years), and the cortex (dating back about one million years). Each layer is interconnected with the previous layer, and any layer can dominate the other layers.

In the following pages we will be seeing how the great storytellers related their magnificent stories to the functions of the brain. They understood how the brain works and what is seeks. They created their stories to satisfy what the brain is searching for. It was this ability that lifted an everyday teller of stories to the level of a master storyteller, just as you will become by the end of this book.

Our first task is to look at the brain and how it evolved.

And so to the brain ... the quick scientific tour. We now look at each layer and its properties:

The brainstem

The midbrain

The cortex

The brainstem

The first evidence of a brain was found 500 million years ago. It is a brain that you find in crocodiles and lizards. It consisted of a brainstem and a spinal cord. The limbs of this creature were stiff, its movements slow, and its requirements minimal. The brainstem brain was pretty limited. It responded to bodily needs, such as hunger and thirst. It knew when to hide when a large object approached or when a loud sound boomed. Every event was a new event. There was no recollection of past events. A loud bang now produced the same reaction to a loud bang a few seconds later. There was no learning. This creature was only geared for survival. It understood pain: lack of food, thirst, and being attacked. It understood pleasure: nice food, warmth, and safety. Pain and pleasure were the brainstem's concerns. We still have a brainstem and all its functions.

The midbrain

After millions of years the body evolved limbs that became more refined. The creature was able to move more freely, climb trees, and travel greater distances. As the creature became more mobile the possible dangers to its survival increased. Reacting to every sensory threat – large animal, loud noise, hot surface, etc. – was consuming too much energy. So evolution added the midbrain. It had all been too much for the brainstem to cope with. The brainstem needed help. It came with the addition of the midbrain.

This combination of brainstem and midbrain was found in creatures that existed 200 million years ago.

The midbrain has a section that warns the creature of possible threats, a sort of red alert button (the amygdala). This part of the brain is connected to the senses: sight, hearing, touch, smell, and taste. Instead of the creature reacting immediately the red alert button would consult a database of dangerous threats (the hippocampus). If the present situation matched the database's record of dangerous situations the brain would signal that action was required. If there was no match the brain would signal that it would be all right to relax.

This midbrain was even more intricate. If the present situation did find a match it would alert an action button (hypothalamus). This action button would send signals to the body to do something: run or fight. Fight or flight: do anything to get back to normal. The creature could now decide, make a choice. Does this scenario pose a threat and does the creature need to do something to eliminate the threat? Or does this scenario not pose a threat and can the creature stay calm?

Time moved on. More and more creatures were born. It became hard not to bump into somebody. And so society emerged. People, people, people. Everybody wanted something. The brain needed help. The brainstem plus midbrain combination needed an upgrade. It was unfit for purpose.

The cortex

So, one million years ago, another part of the brain was added: the cortex. The cortex, in combination with the brainstem and midbrain, was able to cope with social and cultural needs. It had a part that separated man from a mammal. This part was found in the prefrontal cortices. Because mankind now possessed prefrontal cortices it was able to hold one thought in a working memory and then compare that one thought with many other thoughts: hence the development of language, where the symbols representing letters could be combined with sound to form words and language. When making a decision one problem could be compared with many solutions.

Mankind was becoming pretty spectacular, but with one tiny flaw. This potentially huge brain is too big to pass through the birth canal, so there had to be a compromise. The basic structure of the brain and body would be given to the newborn babe at birth. After that the individual, the family, and the family's society would help develop the child's brain.

The brain grows as it assimilates the rules and norms of its society, through its own experiences and through listening to the experiences of others. We truly are a combination of what our birth gives us (nature) and what our society teaches us (nurture/environment).

We conclude this chapter with the reminder that your audience is a complex human being. The master storytellers knew how the brain worked, how mankind was built to survive, and that death and life-threatening incidents would always grab their attention. Join these creators and write a story that could make you rich.

Chapter 17

The end ... not really: every story needs that something extra

You have come to the end of your journey.

You have spotted the formula in all the great tales:

- The evil character (BAD) does (action) something (goal) to harm the good character (GOOD).
- Deep down there is a reason (motivation) why BAD does this.
- The good character (GOOD) reacts and wants to defeat BAD.
- GOOD is involved in many mini episodes that may or may not relate to the ultimate goal.
- Each GOOD mini episode has its own goal, motivation, and actions.
- GOOD finally wins (sometimes loses).

We started our journey together wondering what the master storytellers knew that we did not. You have discovered that our primitive instincts cannot be denied or ignored. We have a body, we are in an environment, and we have a highly evolved brain.

Their spellbinding stories always revolved around the creature that chose evil versus the creature that chose good. This is a lesson for us all. There are people, beings, places, and things involved in your story. Your success will depend on choosing the right combination. Only then might you write the story that could make you rich.

References

1. Lisa Cron, *Wired for Story: The Writer's Guide to Using Brain Science to Hook Readers from the Very First Sentence*, Ten Speed Press, USA, 2012.

2. Annette Simmons, *The Story Factor: Inspiration, Influence, and Persuasion Through the Art of Storytelling*, Basic Books, New York, 2001.

3. Jonathan Gottschall, *The Storytelling Animal: How Stories Make Us Human*, Mariner Books, USA, 2013.

4. Bobette Buster, *DO/STORY: How to Tell Your Story So the World Listens*, The Do Book Company, London, 2013.

5. Nancy Lamb, *The Art and Craft of Storytelling: A Comprehensive Guide to Classic Writing Techniques*, Writer's Digest Books, USA, 2008.

6. Christopher Booker, *The Seven Basic Plots: Why We Tell Stories*, Bloomsbury Continuum, London 2006.

7. Joseph Campbell, *The Hero with a Thousand Faces*, New World Library, California 2008.

8. Horst Kornberger, *The Power of Stories*, Floris Books, Edinburgh 2013.

9. Christopher Vogler, *The Writer's Journey: Mythic Structure for Writers*, Michael Wiese Productions, Studio City 2007.

10. Nancy Mellon, *Storytelling with Children*, Hawthorn Press, UK, 2000.

11. Ashley Ramsden and Sue Hollingsworth, *The Storyteller's Way*, Hawthorn Press, UK, 2013.

12. Michael Wilson, *Flash Writing*, Virtualbookworm.com Publishing, USA, 2004.

13. Luis Cubero, *Business Storytelling Guide*, Intracon, USA, 2014.

14. Doug Lipman, *Improving Your Storytelling*, August House Publishers, USA, 1999.

15. Paul Smith, *Lead with a Story*, AMACOM, USA, 2012.

16. David J Linden, *The Accidental Mind: How Brain Evolution Has Given Us Love, Memory, Dreams, and God*, The Belknap Press of Harvard University Press, USA, 2008.

17. Antonio Damasio *Descartes' Error*, Vintage Books, London, 2006.

18. Jonah Lehrer, *The Decisive Moment: How the Brain Makes Up Its Mind*, Canongate, London, 2009.

19. Susan Greenfield, *The Private Life of the Brain*, Penguin Books, London, 2000.

20. Michael O'Shea, *The Brain: A Very Short Introduction*, Oxford University Press, Oxford, 2005.

21. Neil Shubin, *Your Inner Fish: The amazing discovery of our 375-million-year-old ancestor*, Penguin Books, London, 2008.

ABOUT THE AUTHOR

Paul Larkin is the author of *Fairy Tale Mysteries: Discover the hidden meaning of classical tale*s and *How to Create a Short Story Quickly and Easily: Discover the secret formula used by the master storytellers to get the attention of their audience*. He lives in London, and loves educating and inspiring other authors and storytellers to succeed and to live the life of their dreams.

ONE LAST THING...

If you enjoyed this book or found it useful I'd be very grateful if you'd post a short review on Amazon. Your support really does make a difference, and I read all the reviews personally so I can get your feedback and make this book even better.

Thanks again for your support!